THE JEWEL IN MUMBAI

Bikram Dandiya

Pariyatti Press

Namo tassa bhagavato arahato samma sambuddhassa
Namo tassa bhagavato arahato samma sambuddhassa
Namo tassa bhagavato arahato samma sambuddhassa

Dedicated to

My Mother
My Father
Dhamma Father Goenkaji
Dhamma Mother Mataji

Pariyatti Press
an imprint of
Pariyatti Publishing
www.pariyatti.org

First Edition, 2023

ISBN: 978-1-68172-592-5 (paperback)

Contents

Endorsements

"In this small booklet, meditator-jeweler Bikram Dandiya invites his readers to an enchanted place for Vipassana meditators. He provides a snapshot into the procurement, sculpting, and mounting of the extraordinary crystal that sits at the summit of the remarkable Global Vipassana Pagoda. Bikram's anecdote is clear and personal, making the readers feel as if they are listening to an old friend tell a story over a cup of masala chai. Anyone who delights in meditation, architecture and aesthetics will enjoy this read."

Kory Goldberg

"If one thought that the journey of the construction of the Global Vipassana Pagoda as an architectural marvel was awe inspiring, the story of the crystal is the icing on the cake. Difficulties and challenges were overcome with surrender to Dhamma and the relentless pursuit of the goal of completing this historic monument. This is one more story of the mysterious ways that Dhamma is reawakening in more and more people. Kudos to Bikramji for his contribution."

Nirmala Ganla

Foreword

The Global Vipassana Pagoda in Mumbai was built to mark the birth centenary year of Sayagyi U Ba Khin, the Burmese Dhamma teacher of Shri Satya Narayan Goenkaji. The monument is built in the Myanmar style of the Shwedagon pagoda, as a token of gratitude to that country where the essence of the Buddha's teachings was maintained in its pristine purity, and from where it is now spreading throughout India, and via India to the rest of the world. Our Dhamma teacher Shri S.N. Goenkaji became the vehicle to make this happen. He was also our inspiring guide for every important aspect of this building project. Tremendous volition and effort went into the building of this staggering monument and it is interesting and educative to explore the journey.

Mr. Bikram Dandiya has beautifully chronicled some of these experiences in his booklet, "The Jewel in Mumbai", the story of the making of the crystal bud atop the Global Vipassana Pagoda. Although his story concentrates on a specific part of this enormous structure, it typifies the challenges and solutions witnessed by those of us closely involved in its creation. For example, experts had opined that it was not possible to construct a 325 foot wide stone dome without supporting pillars; the dome went up thanks to indigenous technology, using thousands of huge interlocking stones weighing 700 to 800 kg each, and now seemingly floating in the air!

The story of the crystal shows how Dhamma works, and we at the Global Vipassana Foundation wish to continue sharing the anecdotes of history relating to various aspects of the building of the Global Vipassana Pagoda – the gems that have strung together this gigantic yet delicately intricate monument.

My best wishes to Bikram Dandiyaji, and my appreciation for his contribution towards the making of the crystal crowning the Global Vipassana Pagoda. May all beings be happy, peaceful, and liberated.

M.M. Khandhar, 14th January 2020

Preamble

I was first encouraged to document the creation of the crystal bud at the Global Vipassana Pagoda by Khandharji, the Centre Teacher of Dhamma Pattana Vipassana Centre, located in the Global Vipassana Pagoda premises. There was recurring curiosity about this subject amongst his students and visitors, and I mailed him an essay on it several years back. Then, quite recently, I visited the Global Vipassana Pagoda again after a gap of over 5 years, to attend a workshop on the Bhikkhu Vinaya.

On the last day of my stay some young servers discovered that I had a part to play in the creation of the crystal bud, and this initiated excited interest and curiosity on the subject. I left early next morning with a determination to document relevant information and photos for posterity, which I've attempted to do in this little book. While documenting I've tried to bring alive the small 'miracles' that occurred during this journey; I hope the reader finds them inspiring.

At this same workshop Shri Manjappaji, the main speaker, was asked to shed light on the relevance of mounting crystals on top of pagodas. He explained it as follows: the base of the pagoda, which is big and broad, represents *sīla*, the rings near the summit represent *samādhi*, and the crystal on top represents *nibbāna*. In the over 15 years since I worked with this crystal bud for the Global Vipassana Pagoda, this is the best explanation about their relevance that I have heard.

All along the process of making this crystal bud my thankfulness towards Guruji, for having allowed me this rare opportunity, kept competing with the sheer excitement of actually doing the job. Reflecting back, I feel only immense gratitude, and a wonderful feeling of satisfaction, thanks to this one great man.

Bikram Dandiya
26th January, 2020

A Sadhuvaad

ग्लोबल पगोडा पर गुम्बज का निर्माण

मुझे याद हैं पूज्य गोयनकाजी की हार्दिक इच्छा थी कि ग्लोबल पगोडा पर प्रस्तावित गुम्बज नेचुरल क्रिस्टल में ही तैयार हो, क्यों कि काँच में वो बात नहीं होती । इसके लिये उन्होंने बिक्रमजी डांडिया को प्रेरणा दी, बल्कि वे खुद ही प्रेरित हो गए और जब खोज शुरू करी तो पता चला कि इस तरह का एक बड़ा रफ़ क्रिस्टल संभवतः ब्राज़ील (दक्षिण अमेरिका) में उपलब्ध हैं, तो बिक्रमजी वहाँ भी जाने के लिये तैयार हो गये । पर जब जानकारी मिली की वो 200 से 225 किलो का रफ़ क्रिस्टल संयोग वश जयपुर ही पहुँच चुका हैं, तो इन्होंने ठान लिया कि इसको ज़रूर ख़रीदना हैं और उनका प्रयास जारी रहा । इसके आगे कि यात्रा तो इस किताब में, जो कि बहुत ही रोचक बन पड़ी हैं, में लिखा हुआ हैं कि - कैसे संयोगवश इतना बड़ा क्रिस्टल मिला और गुम्बज का निर्माण कैसे हुआ ?

मैं समझता हूँ कि इस सम्पूर्ण प्रक्रिया में धर्म की पूरी मदद मिली हैं । आज यह गुम्बज इतना बड़ा हैं कि दूर से ही नज़र आता हैं अन्यथा तो इतने विशाल पगोडा पर छोटे से क्रिस्टल का पता ही नहीं चलता । यह पुस्तक यही बताती हैं कि इतना बड़ा साफ़ सुथरा क्रिस्टल मिलना कितना आश्चर्यजनक था । भविष्य में जब तक यह विशाल ग्लोबल पगोडा क़ायम रहेगा तब तक यह बात स्मरणीये रहेगी ।

मेरा डांडिया जी को बहुत-बहुत साधुवाद, जिन्होंने इतने बड़े काम को पूरा किया साथ ही आपके पिताश्री को भी फ़क्र होगा कि इस तरह का एक ऐतिहासिक गुम्बज ग्लोबल पगोडा के शीर्ष पर लगा हैं जिसमें आपका बहुमूल्य योगदान हैं ।

अनेकों मंगल कामनाएँ ।

विमल चन्द सुराना

17-8-20

Acknowledgments

(English Translation of Suranaji Letter on Previous Page)

I remember that Pujya Goenkaji sincerely wished that the Global Vipassana Pagoda be crowned with a natural crystal bud. Bikram Dandiyaji got inspired to present this piece to the pagoda. When the search began, it was rumoured that one such large rough crystal piece was available in Brazil. As Bikramji was preparing to visit Brazil, it was rumoured that the 200 kg crystal had been brought to Jaipur for sale; Bikramji decided that it must be procured.

The rest of the story is presented in this booklet in a very interesting manner: how through the synchronicity of circumstances such an unusually large specimen of rough crystal, which was clean and clear, was procured, processed and delivered to the top of the Global Vipassana Pagoda; the Global Vipassana Pagoda is so large that a smaller crystal bud would have been lost to sight! It is my understanding that Dhamma has fully helped this entire process.

This booklet ensures that these interesting details will be available for posterity; till such time that the Global Vipassana Pagoda exists.

I extend my *sadhuvad* to Dandiyaji for fulfilling this wholesome task. It is my belief that Dandiyaji's father will also be very proud of the historic achievement of installing this precious crystal on the pinnacle of this grand Global Vipassana Pagoda.

Vimal Chand Surana
16th August 2020, Jaipur

From the
Chalangadana Sutta AN 6.37

On one occasion the Buddha was staying near Sravasti at Jetavana. On that occasion he extolled the six factors that make for a good donation, of which three of the factors apply to the donors and the other three apply to the recipients. And which are the three factors applying to the donors? They are where the donors:

before giving are glad,
while giving their mind is bright & clear,
and after having given, feel uplifted.

And which are the three factors applying to the recipients?
Where the recipients are:

free of passion or are practicing for the subduing of passion,
free of aversion or are practicing for the subduing of aversion,
and free of delusion or are practicing for the subduing of delusion.

It's not easy to grasp the merit of such an offering...
it is simply reckoned as an incalculable, immeasurable, great mass of merit, unquantifiable like the water in the great ocean.

THE JEWEL IN MUMBAI

THE GLOBAL VIPASSANA PAGODA

CRYSTAL STORY

The Story

The story of the Global Vipassana Pagoda crystal began around the winter of 2001 when Bob Jeffs of Canada and I had taken on the task of fixing the light underneath the crystal that crowns the Dhamma Giri pagoda. Guruji had apparently told Premji Savla that this would make the *devis* and *devatas* here very happy. Meanwhile, at Mumbai work on the Global Vipassana Pagoda had started. It occurred to me that there would be a need for a crystal there at some point in time, as all the pagodas I had seen were capped by a crystal. Being a jeweller, on my next visit to Jaipur, out of curiosity, I asked a rough–gem broker where the best crystal would be found.

I was informed that a Jaipur dealer has a very good specimen at his Brazil warehouse, but we would have to visit Brazil to see it, while the price quoted was more than what I could afford. During my next visit to Dhamma Giri I mustered up the courage to address Guruji and Mataji during one of their evening walks. They didn't know me then and belying the price being demanded for the crystal, a strange courage prompted me to seek their permission to provide the crystal for the Global Vipassana Pagoda; Guruji paused for a few moments, looked at me keenly and asked if I could arrange for the money to which I said yes.

When I enquired from Guruji how big the crystal would need to be, following a moment of reflection he replied that it should be about 'two and a half feet' to which I said OK and with a supportive blessing from Mataji, I withdrew with folded hands.

When back in Jaipur in April 2002, I excitedly called the broker, Omji, to make further enquiries about the Brazilian crystal. To my delight I was informed that we no longer needed to visit Brazil as the crystal had been brought to Jaipur for sale, and because no good offers had been forthcoming the price had been halved. This was very encouraging, so we arranged an appointment to visit the owner, who I was yet to meet. I also requested Abi Miyan, an expert gemstone carver who I had previously worked with, to come along and give his expert opinion on the quality of the piece, as rough gemstones can be very deceptive to the untrained eye.

As we entered the dealer's residence–cum–office compound, Abi Miyan noticed a large rough whitish stone parked unpretentiously on the lawn outside near a plant pot. It looked very weather worn and modest. Abi remarked "I think this is the piece, and if so, it is good".

Looking at the piece it was hard to be convinced, but then Abi was the expert. As we entered the dealer's office, I saw Bipin Jhalani, a classmate of mine from school, who as it turned out was the owner! In this new atmosphere of familiar conviviality, when I told Bipin where the crystal was destined for, he was happy to sell the rough crystal at a quarter of his original asking price, an amount I could afford! I was overjoyed that in spite of my limited resources the project could move forward! How it is, when we have a Dhamma volition, all the positive forces come in support to make the unexpected happen!

The Rough Crystal

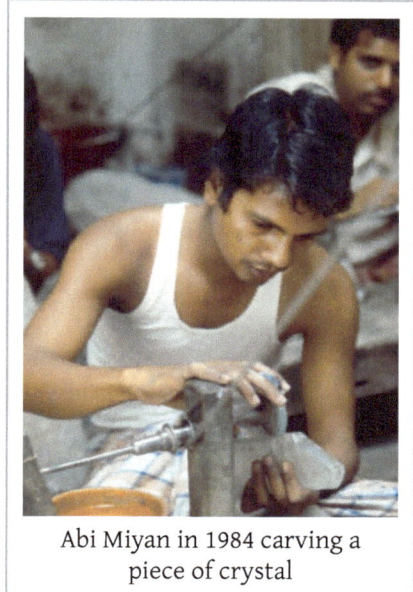

Abi Miyan in 1984 carving a
piece of crystal

Meanwhile Abi Miyan had gathered a small pile of rough 'tourmaline' gemstones, winked at me suggesting that we buy that pile of stones as well, and with a poker faced demeanour concealing his enthusiasm from Bipin, settled a price with him. I was hesitant at paying out any more money, however little, and specially for these unconvincing stones, but was admonished by a sharp look from Abi.

He also found a moment to whisper in my ear that he would buy them all from me and I should really keep some for myself, while one big black one was specially for him. OK! As it turned out, the profit from this inconsequentially priced small collection of rough gemstones, was to reimburse the entire cost of the pagoda crystal, with much more money left over!

The rough tourmaline from the selected pile

People usually press me to 'please tell us the cost of the crystal', and my answer, with a smile, is always and truthfully 'nothing'! Here is a very tangible demonstration of Guruji's advice to us: when we give *dāna* we are deprived of 'nothing'! We brought home our bounty, and Abi appeared next morning to pick up the black piece, which against the sun, revealed itself to be a deep desirable red!

A tiny piece of this rough red tourmaline, which I pressed upon Abi to return to me, has recently served as the sample piece for my daughter Kichu's gem cutting initiation; we were startled by the quality of the finished piece and its current market valuation.

Finished jewelery pieces from gems originating from the tourmaline pile

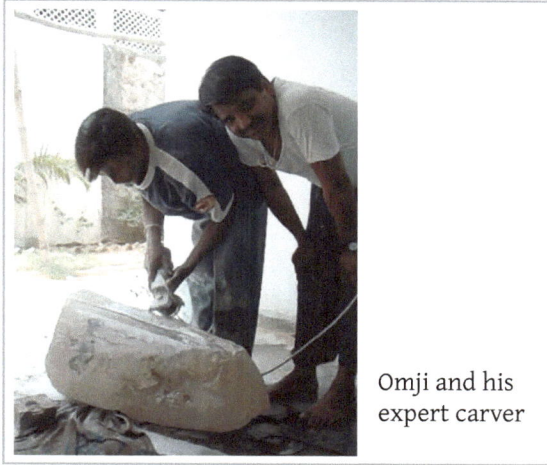

Omji and his
expert carver

Omji and I took the big crystal rough to a local granite cutting workshop in order to have it shaped, as he didn't have the large machinery required. Soon after we began slicing off an extra surface layer, Omji who is normally a very calm person, got visibly excited! He could detect how clean and white the interior of the crystal really was! Later I was offered a sizable sum of money for this extra layer, almost matching the full cost of the 200 kg stone itself, I preferred instead to keep it. It was later carved with the scene of the Tathagata at Isipatana instructing his 55 disciples to go in all directions.

I was hoping to present this carving to Guruji, but as it took several years to finish and came together too late this could not happen.

The original crystal for the pagoda stone was initially shaped at my house by one of Omji's craftsmen, which itself was a minor miracle as such craftsmen are very hard to come by and therefore very carefully protected by their employers. Once shaped, we presented Guruji with a drawing of how we visualised the surface carving to look. This was an untraditional design from the Burmese perspective, and Guruji sent the drawing to Burma for approval. Aleksei Gomez from Venezuela, then living at Dhamma Giri, had rendered the design on paper for us.

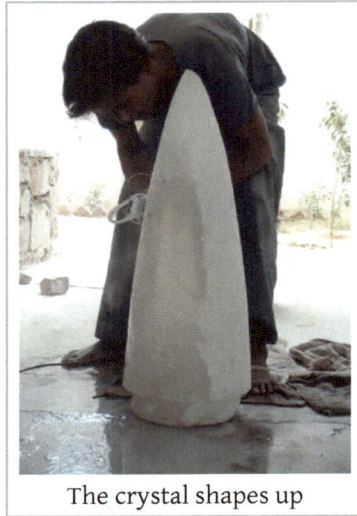

The crystal shapes up

This new design has now become the new standard for all the crystals going up at Vipassana pagodas in India and abroad, and is also being appreciated by traditional monasteries such as the famous Na Uyana monastery in Sri Lanka where one such piece adorns their pagoda. Once the design was approved by Guruji's Burmese advisors, the piece went to Omji's own workshop to be finished off and polished, and our finished crystal emerged to be 30 inches tall, quite miraculously complying with Guruji's specifications.

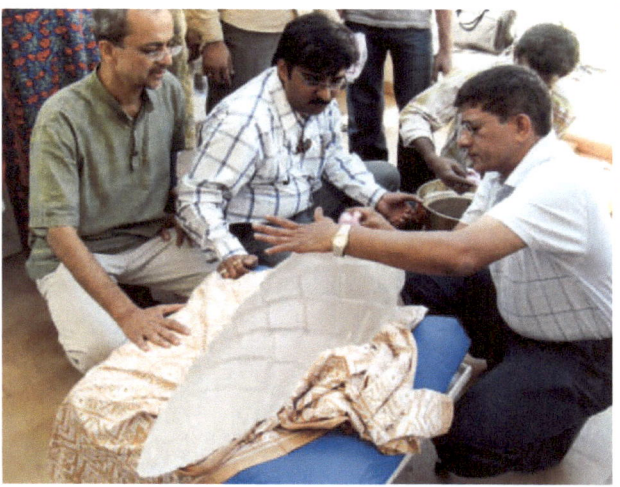

The crystal being packed for its journey to Mumbai

Next came the question of its transportation to Mumbai. Ramnath Shenoy, who lived in Mumbai, was my colleague in this leg of the exercise. On his own initiative he negotiated a deal with an airline to air freight it, while I was exploring train and road options, preferring not to let the piece out of sight as far as possible. One evening, out of the blue, I received a call from Ramnath saying that he was to visit Jaipur the very next morning on an emergency visit to his head office, which coincidentally, happened to be in Jaipur. He arrived at my house straight from the airport, but before he could visit his office he received a call cancelling his emergency meeting. So here he was in Jaipur, at the disposal of the crystal, and we had the day to pursue our objective of getting the crystal to Mumbai. The airline declined to take the crystal up on short notice, and later that evening we were at the railway station, trying to book the crystal as unattended baggage (packed now in a strong wooden box upholstered in blue velvet) on the train. But they wouldn't have it as the crystal weighed 80 kg, exceeding their maximum limit by 10 kg.

Then a very strange thing happened: as travellers on the route know, there is only a negligible chance of getting a last minute passenger reservation on a Jaipur-Mumbai train, but as we were at the station, we enquired. To our surprise the clerk issued us a confirmed ticket on the spot! Exuberant, we proceeded to the coach debating how we would place the crystal. We would not like to keep it on the floor, and it would be too obtrusive on the berth, potentially inviting objections from fellow passengers. As we entered the coach, there was a strange silence inside. It soon dawned on us that we were the only people on this AC coach of 70 berths; this coach had been added to the train at the last minute, and Ramnath travelled all alone in it to Mumbai, with the brahmin ticket inspector keeping him company and thanking him for the opportunity of being able to pray near the crystal through the night.

Dhamma works!

Crystal reaches Mumbai

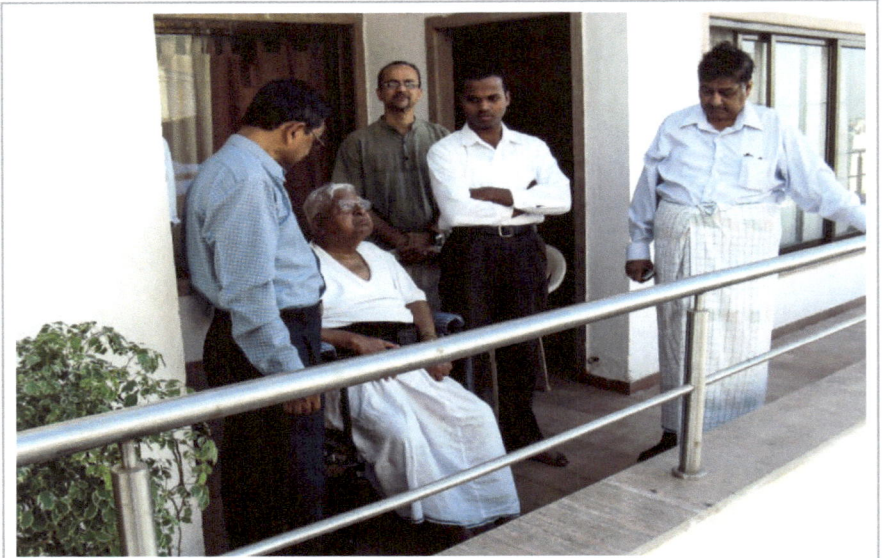

Guruji looking up at the top of the pagoda where the crystal was to be housed

Our next big surprise came at the inauguration of the pagoda when the crystal was to be mounted right on top, at a date and time prescribed by Guruji's Burmese contacts. This was a big event for which the President of India, our chief guest, was being flown in, and the date and time were parallel with her arrival on the site. However, it was decided locally that in view of this momentous event, the crystal would go up the evening before the appointed date. Attempts were made to do so, but they failed: the crystal went up to the top of the pagoda, but could not be mounted for one reason or another.

Early next morning we tried to continue with our task, but again our attempts failed; the crystal went up only as the President's helicopter landed on the clearing made for it nearby, at the exact time designated for its mounting by our Burmese advisors! Nayanbhai Shah and I, having placed the crystal on its mount, came down to the inner pagoda exhilarated, just as the formal inaugural proceedings commenced. Here I joined my father who had arrived from Jaipur to attend the event.

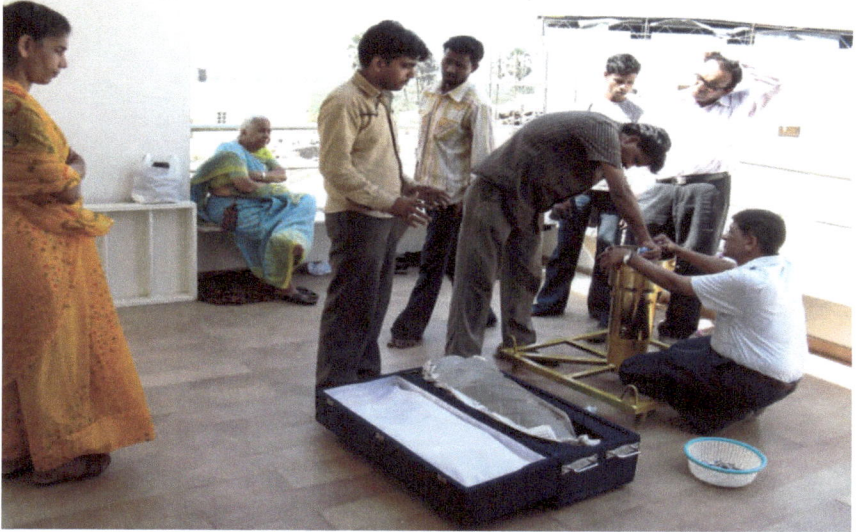

Crystal mount being prepared

Crystal being circumambulated reverentially around the pagoda on a palanquin specially prepared for it

Guruji and Mataji blessing the crystal just before its journey
to the top of the pagoda

The crystal completes its journey and is finally mounted on the
top of the pagoda

Shri Ram Singhji and Shri Gopal Singhji and their families posing for a picture with the crystal

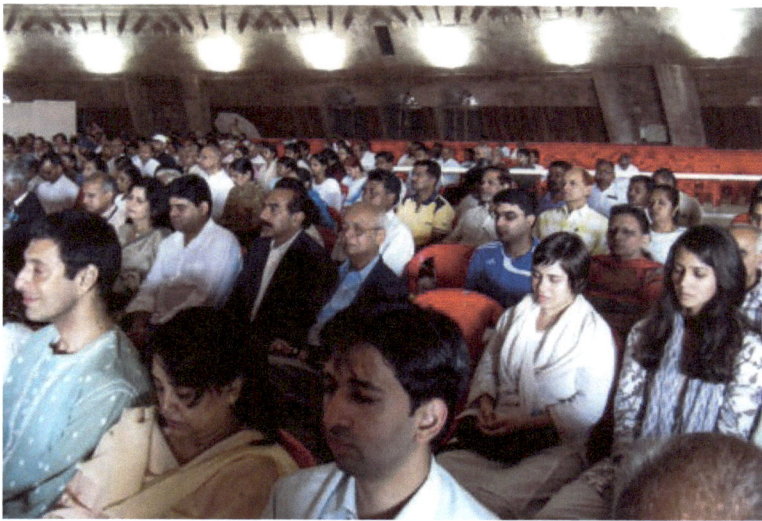

Some of the participants at the inauguration

This is the story of a small jeweller's volition to put up this big crystal 325 feet high up on the Mumbai skyline, over the largest pagoda to be built in recent years! On a certain occasion during these events even Guruji expressed his pleasant surprise on this opportunity that I had received, albeit through his good office! My take on these events is this crystal was to reach the top of the pagoda regardless; by my Dhamma volition and efforts I became one amongst the many instruments for the progression of this event.

Having done so, the inexplicable small miracles that facilitated this event strengthened my *shraddha* (devotion) further, while I was fortunate to earn merits of *dāna* in the process. Remembering this good fortune that came my way, I share whatever merits earned with those who made this possible, starting with Guruji and Mataji and all the chain of teachers not yet liberated, with my parents and ancestors, and with all those that helped me fulfil this task in whichever way; with you all that have read through this story, with my daughter, relatives and friends, and with all beings!

Reverend Bhikkhu Sangha with the crystal at a ceremony preceding the impending mounting of the crystal on top of the Global Vipassana Pagoda, and thus signifying its completion.

The author (far right) with Guruji, Mataji, and some meditators, with the crystal and pagoda in the background.

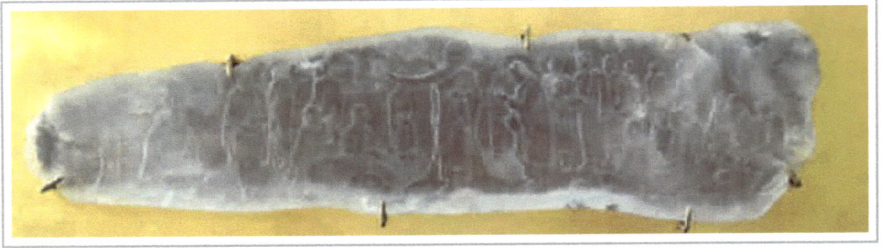

The extra layer of crystal that was removed from the original piece, which went on top of the pagoda, was later carved into this historical scene: The Buddha at Isipatana (Sarnath) instructing his 55 disciples to go in all directions to teach The Dhamma *"bahujana hitaya, bahujana sukhaya, lokanukampaya"*, for the good of many, for the well being of many, out of compassion for the world.

The Crystal Management Team at Global Pagoda. Left to right: Sameer Patel, Bikram Dandiya, Unidentified Person, Deepak Pagare, Dhananjay Chavan, Ramnath Shenoy

It Doesn't End There....

In August 2020, as the first edition of this booklet was going into print, I delivered the remaining pieces of the rough-green-tourmaline pile for a clearance sale to Abi Miyan. These were the remnants of what he had so propitiously nudged me into buying. He now surprised me by making an amazing offer for the waste pieces of the over 200 kg crystal that was reduced to the 80 kg Global Vipassana Pagoda bud. These ranged from tiny shards to some larger pieces of up to 12 inches in length.

These 'waste pieces' had been lying safely in a strong room ever since 2005, although they constituted no commercial value at that time. However, I had held on to them on a hunch. I even commissioned some beads from them, which were subsequently strung into 2 necklaces finished off in gold. These were made with the intent of offering them to Guruji who I imagined might want to present them to appropriate dignitaries at the time of the inauguration of the Global Vipassana Pagoda. However, these were not given to anyone on Guruji's admonishment.

Sadly for Abi, I turned his 2020 offer down. He has since repeated this offer twice, the second one being as recently as in 2022. I am now looking out for the construction of a sacred structure, such as a pagoda, conveniently close by to Jaipur into which I can enshrine these remnants.

It is really fascinating how the results of a happily made *dāna* are so multi-dimensional that even the ordinary becomes extraordinary, and even the 'valueless' becomes invaluable.

What Is a Crystal?

'Crystal' is a term applying to a wide variety of solids, natural or man made. For our purpose, a it refers to a clean white natural quartz colloquially called 'rock crystal'. The chemical structure of Quartz is silicon and oxygen atoms arranged in a highly ordered repeating pattern in the SiO_4 formula. A 'rock crystal' is multifaceted and tapers to a point at the top. They are mostly opaque at the base, getting progressively clearer as they go up. Good sized natural rock crystals can take millions of years to form.

Rock crystals are found in many parts of the world. However most are of little value or use as they can be tiny, opaque, discoloured, and not hard enough to take a good polish. Even for a small pagoda bud a suitable rock crystal would ideally be about ten kilos in weight, a foot in length, white, hard and clear; the so called 'crystal clear'. The enhancement of the above five factors make a crystal progressively rarer. To draw an analogy human beings are found the world over, but to find a human being that observes the five *sīla* in their purity is rare. The crystal used for the bud topping the Global Vipassana Pagoda is indeed such a rare crystal. A comparable crystal has yet to be traced.

Once procured a crystal is carved into a bud like shape. Thereafter the bud is ground down progressively to a very smooth and transparent glass like finish. The removal of the excess material from the surface by carving could be compared to the removal of the five *nīvaraṇa* in the development of *samādhi*. The progressive grinding down leading to the final polish can be looked upon as the progressive development of *paññā* leading to the supreme fruit of *nibbāna*.

A lot of esoteric and other-worldly properties are associated with rock crystals making them valuable from time immemorial.

Relics of the Buddhas have often been found preserved in crystal caskets. Burmese and Sri Lankan pagodas have traditionally been topped by them.

Plenty of facts support their desirability in other realms as well. Kings and queens have eaten and drunk from rock crystal receptacles and have worn crowns adorned by them. Furthermore many religious traditions have used crystals in representing their deities and sacred artifacts.

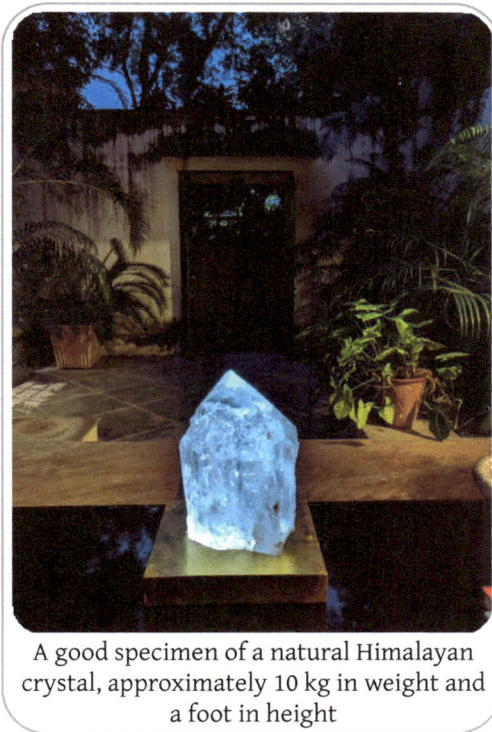

A good specimen of a natural Himalayan crystal, approximately 10 kg in weight and a foot in height

The author wants to express his gratitude for his role in the incorporation of the crystal at the Global Vipassana Pagoda, Mumbai.
He does not seek any commercial benefit or personal gain from the book.
Send your feedback to Bikram Dandiya (bikram.dandiya@dhamma.org).

ABOUT VIPASSANA

Courses of Vipassana meditation as taught by S.N. Goenka in the tradition of Sayagyi U Ba Khin are held regularly in many countries around the world.

Information, worldwide schedules and application forms are available from the Vipassana website: www.dhamma.org.

ABOUT PARIYATTI

Pariyatti is dedicated to providing affordable access to authentic teachings of the Buddha about the Dhamma theory (*pariyatti*) and practice (*paṭipatti*) of Vipassana meditation. A 501(c)(3) nonprofit charitable organization since 2002, Pariyatti is sustained by contributions from individuals who appreciate and want to share the incalculable value of the Dhamma teachings. We invite you to visit www.pariyatti.org to learn about our programs, services, and ways to support publishing and other undertakings.

Pariyatti Publishing Imprints

Vipassana Research Publications (focus on Vipassana as taught by S.N. Goenka in the tradition of Sayagyi U Ba Khin)

BPS Pariyatti Editions (selected titles from the Buddhist Publication Society, copublished by Pariyatti)

MPA Pariyatti Editions (selected titles from the Myanmar Pitaka Association, copublished by Pariyatti)

Pariyatti Digital Editions (audio and video titles, including discourses)

Pariyatti Press (classic titles returned to print and inspirational writing by contemporary authors)

Pariyatti enriches the world by
- disseminating the words of the Buddha,
- providing sustenance for the seeker's journey,
- illuminating the meditator's path.